AF486929

THE ART OF SELF-DISCOVERY

A JOURNEY TO FINDING YOUR TRUE SELF

VIPUL BAIBHAV

Copyright © Vipul Baibhav
All Rights Reserved.

This book has been self-published with all reasonable efforts taken to make the material error-free by the author. No part of this book shall be used, reproduced in any manner whatsoever without written permission from the author, except in the case of brief quotations embodied in critical articles and reviews.

The Author of this book is solely responsible and liable for its content including but not limited to the views, representations, descriptions, statements, information, opinions and references ["Content"]. The Content of this book shall not constitute or be construed or deemed to reflect the opinion or expression of the Publisher or Editor. Neither the Publisher nor Editor endorse or approve the Content of this book or guarantee the reliability, accuracy or completeness of the Content published herein and do not make any representations or warranties of any kind, express or implied, including but not limited to the implied warranties of merchantability, fitness for a particular purpose. The Publisher and Editor shall not be liable whatsoever for any errors, omissions, whether such errors or omissions result from negligence, accident, or any other cause or claims for loss or damages of any kind, including without limitation, indirect or consequential loss or damage arising out of use, inability to use, or about the reliability, accuracy or sufficiency of the information contained in this book.

Made with ♥ on the Notion Press Platform
www.notionpress.com

"To all those who seek to understand themselves and their place in the world, may this book be a guide on your journey of self-discovery. To my family and friends, thank you for your constant support and encouragement. And to my own self, for being my biggest teacher."

This book is dedicated to those who have the courage to look within themselves, to confront their fears, and to embrace their true selves. It is for those who are ready to take responsibility for their lives and to make positive changes. May this book be a source of inspiration and a tool for personal growth and development.

To my parents, for their unwavering love and support throughout my journey, and for teaching me the importance of self-discovery. And to my partner, for being my constant companion on this journey, and for helping me to see the beauty in myself. This book is for all of you.

To all those who have been a part of my journey, the ones who have supported me, the ones who have challenged me, the ones who have helped me grow. This book is my way of expressing my gratitude, and my way of giving back. May it serve as a reminder that we all have the power to shape our own lives and to become the best version of ourselves.

"To the readers, I hope this book will serve as a guide on your journey of self-discovery, to help you understand yourself better, to empower you to make positive changes, and to inspire you to live your life to the fullest."

Contents

Foreword

In this fast-paced world where we are constantly on the go, it can be easy to lose sight of who we are and what we want out of life. Vipul Baibhav's book, "The Art of Self-Discovery: A Journey to Finding Your True Self," offers a much-needed reminder to take a step back, to reflect, and to understand ourselves better. Through practical techniques and strategies, this book guides readers on a journey of self-discovery and personal growth.

As you read through the pages of this book, you will be led on a journey of self-awareness, self-acceptance, and self-compassion. The author's approach is both honest and relatable, providing readers with the tools and resources they need to understand themselves and make positive changes in their lives.

I highly recommend this book to anyone who is looking to improve their personal and professional lives. Whether you are a student, a working professional, or a retiree, this book will offer valuable insights and practical advice to help you achieve your goals.

Vipul Baibhav has done a great job in providing a comprehensive guide to help readers discover themselves, build emotional and mental resilience, set goals and achieve them. The book is well-structured, easy to read and understand with practical examples and actionable steps. It is a must-read for anyone looking to improve themselves and live a fulfilling life.

In short, this book is a valuable resource for anyone looking to improve themselves and their lives. I encourage you to read it with an open mind and to take the time to reflect on the insights and advice it offers. Happy reading!

Preface

In this preface, I want to express my excitement for the publication of my book, "The Art of Self-Discovery: A Journey to Finding Your True Self." This book is the result of many years of research, reflection, and personal experience. It is a culmination of everything I have learned and discovered about myself and the world around me.

Self-discovery is a lifelong journey, and it is not always easy. It requires honesty, courage, and the willingness to look within ourselves and confront our fears. It also requires a willingness to embrace change and to make positive changes in our lives.

This book is intended to be a guide for those who are ready to take the first steps on their journey of self-discovery. It is filled with practical tools and techniques that will help readers to understand themselves better, to set goals, and to make positive changes in their lives.

The book is divided into chapters that cover various aspects of self-discovery, including understanding the mind, self-reflection, self-awareness, self-acceptance, setting goals, and building resilience. Each chapter includes practical examples, actionable steps and exercises that readers can apply to their own lives.

I hope this book will serve as a valuable resource for those who are looking to improve themselves and their lives. I encourage readers to take the time to reflect on the insights and advice it offers and to apply them to their own lives.

Thank you for taking the time to read this book. I wish you all the best on your journey of self-discovery.

Acknowledgements

I would like to express my deepest gratitude to all those who have supported me in the creation of this book.

First, I would like to thank my family and friends for their unwavering support and encouragement. Their belief in me and my abilities has been a constant source of inspiration.

I would also like to thank my editor and publisher for their guidance and expertise in bringing this book to fruition. Their professionalism and dedication have been invaluable.

I am also grateful to the individuals who have shared their stories and experiences with me. Their willingness to be vulnerable and open has helped me to better understand the human experience and to create a more relatable and impactful book.

Finally, I would like to thank all of the readers of this book. It is my hope that the insights and advice shared in this book will help you to improve your personal and professional lives.

Thank you all for your support, encouragement and for being a part of this journey.

Sincerely, Vipul Baibhav.

Prologue

We all have a deep desire to understand ourselves and our place in the world. We want to know who we are and what we want out of life. But for many of us, this journey of self-discovery is not always easy. It can be filled with uncertainty, fear, and self-doubt.

This book is about taking the first steps on the journey of self-discovery. It is about understanding ourselves better, setting goals, and making positive changes in our lives. It is about learning to accept ourselves, to be kind to ourselves, and to build emotional and mental resilience.

Throughout this book, you will be guided through various techniques and strategies to help you understand your thoughts, emotions, and behaviors, and to make positive changes in your life. You will learn to reflect on your past experiences and to set realistic and achievable goals for your future.

This book is not a magic wand that will instantly solve all of your problems. It is a guide, a tool to help you on your journey. It is a reminder that you are not alone, and that you have the power to shape your own life.

As you read through the pages of this book, I encourage you to reflect on your own experiences and to apply the insights and advice it offers to your own life. Remember that self-discovery is a lifelong journey, and it is not always easy, but with the right tools and mindset, you can achieve anything.

So, let's begin the journey together.

CHAPTER ONE

The importance of self-discovery

Self-discovery is the process of understanding oneself and one's place in the world. It is the journey of understanding who we are, what we want out of life, and how to achieve it. It is a lifelong process that requires honesty, courage, and the willingness to look within ourselves and confront our fears.

Self-discovery is important because it helps us to understand ourselves better and to make positive changes in our lives. When we understand ourselves, we can make better decisions, set realistic and achievable goals, and build emotional and mental resilience.

Self-discovery also helps us to understand our strengths, weaknesses, and values. It helps us to identify the things that are important to us, and to make choices that align with our values. This can lead to greater satisfaction and fulfillment in our lives.

Self-discovery also helps us to understand our relationships with others. It helps us to understand how our actions and behaviors affect others, and to build stronger and more meaningful relationships.

In addition, self-discovery is important because it helps us to understand our place in the world. It helps us to understand our role in society and to make a positive impact on the world around us.

In conclusion, self-discovery is a vital aspect of personal growth and development. It helps us to understand ourselves better, make positive changes in our lives, and to live a more fulfilling and meaningful life.

CHAPTER TWO

Understanding the mind

Understanding the mind is an important aspect of self-discovery. The mind is complex and multifaceted, and it can be difficult to understand how it works and how it influences our thoughts, emotions, and behaviors.

The mind is made up of three main components: the conscious mind, the subconscious mind, and the unconscious mind. The conscious mind is the part of the mind that is aware of our thoughts and experiences. The subconscious mind is the part of the mind that stores our memories, emotions, and beliefs. The unconscious mind is the part of the mind that controls our automatic behaviors and processes.

It is important to understand the role that each of these parts of the mind plays in our lives. Our thoughts, emotions, and behaviors are all influenced by the mind. Understanding how the mind works can help us to understand why we think and feel the way we do, and how to make positive changes.

One way to understand the mind is through mindfulness, the practice of paying attention to the present moment. Mindfulness helps us to become more aware of our thoughts and emotions, and to understand how they are influencing our behavior.

Another way to understand the mind is through cognitive-behavioral therapy (CBT), a form of therapy that helps individuals to understand how their thoughts, emotions, and behaviors are interconnected, and how to change negative patterns.

In conclusion, understanding the mind is an important aspect of self-discovery. It helps us to understand how our thoughts, emotions, and behaviors are interconnected, and how to make positive changes in our lives. Mindfulness and cognitive-behavioral therapy are useful tools to help us in this process.

CHAPTER THREE

Self-reflection

Self-reflection is the process of looking within ourselves and evaluating our thoughts, emotions, and behaviors. It is an important aspect of self-discovery, as it helps us to understand ourselves better and to identify patterns and limiting beliefs that may be holding us back.

Self-reflection can be done through journaling, meditating, or talking to a therapist or trusted friend. It is important to approach self-reflection with an open and non-judgmental attitude. By looking at our thoughts and behaviors objectively, we can better understand why we do the things we do, and how to make positive changes.

Self-reflection can also help us to identify our strengths and weaknesses, and to set realistic and achievable goals. By understanding our strengths and weaknesses, we can make better decisions, set goals that align with our values, and build emotional and mental resilience.

It is also important to reflect on past experiences, both positive and negative. Reflecting on past experiences can help us to learn from our mistakes and to identify patterns that may be holding us back.

In conclusion, self-reflection is an important aspect of self-discovery. It helps us to understand ourselves better, identify patterns and limiting beliefs, set realistic and achievable goals, and to learn from our past experiences. Journaling, meditating, or talking to a therapist or trusted friend are useful tools for self-reflection.

CHAPTER FOUR

Self-awareness

Self-awareness is the ability to understand one's own thoughts, emotions, and behaviors. It is an important aspect of self-discovery, as it helps us to understand our strengths, weaknesses, and values.

Self-awareness can be developed through various practices such as mindfulness, meditation, journaling, or therapy. These practices help us to become more aware of our thoughts, emotions, and behaviors and to understand how they influence our lives.

Self-awareness also helps us to identify our triggers, the things that cause us to react emotionally. By understanding our triggers, we can better manage our emotions and avoid unnecessary conflicts.

Self-awareness also helps us to understand our values and to make choices that align with them. By understanding our values, we can make decisions that are in line with what we believe is important, which can lead to greater satisfaction and fulfillment in our lives.

In conclusion, self-awareness is an important aspect of self-discovery. It helps us to understand our strengths, weaknesses, values, triggers and to make choices that align with them. Mindfulness, meditation, journaling, or therapy are useful tools for developing self-awareness.

CHAPTER FIVE

Self-acceptance

Self-acceptance is the ability to accept ourselves, flaws and all. It is an important aspect of self-discovery, as it helps us to build self-esteem and to lead a more fulfilling life.

Self-acceptance starts with understanding that we are all imperfect, and that it is okay to make mistakes. It is important to practice self-compassion, treating ourselves with the same kindness and understanding that we would offer to a friend.

One way to practice self-acceptance is through positive affirmations. These are positive statements that help to counteract negative thoughts and beliefs. For example, "I am worthy of love and acceptance" or "I am capable of achieving my goals".

Another way to practice self-acceptance is through gratitude. By focusing on the things we are thankful for, we can shift our focus away from our flaws and towards the positive aspects of ourselves.

Self-acceptance also includes accepting and embracing our unique qualities and characteristics, rather than constantly striving to be someone else.

In conclusion, self-acceptance is an important aspect of self-discovery. It helps us to build self-esteem, to treat ourselves with kindness and compassion, and to lead a more fulfilling life. Positive affirmations and gratitude are useful tools for practicing self-acceptance.

CHAPTER SIX

Setting goals and creating a plan

Setting goals and creating a plan is an important aspect of self-discovery, as it helps us to focus on what we want to achieve and to make positive changes in our lives.

The process of setting goals begins with identifying our values and what is important to us. This will help us to set goals that align with our values and that will bring us greater satisfaction and fulfillment.

Once we have identified our goals, it is important to create a plan to achieve them. This includes setting specific, measurable, achievable, relevant, and time-bound (SMART) goals. For example, "I want to lose 10 pounds in the next 3 months by exercising at least 30 minutes per day and following a healthy diet."

It is also important to break down our goals into smaller, manageable steps. This will help us to stay focused and motivated, and to track our progress.

Creating a plan also includes identifying any potential obstacles that may arise and creating a strategy to overcome them. This will help us to stay on track, even when things get difficult.

In conclusion, setting goals and creating a plan is an important aspect of self-discovery. It helps us to focus on what we want to achieve, to make positive changes in our lives, and to lead a more fulfilling life. Identifying our values, setting SMART goals and breaking them down into manageable steps, and identifying potential obstacles and creating a strategy to overcome them are all important elements of creating a plan.

CHAPTER SEVEN

Overcoming obstacles

Overcoming obstacles is an important part of life. Whether it's a personal challenge or a professional hurdle, the ability to face and overcome obstacles is key to achieving success and reaching our goals. However, it's not always easy to know how to tackle these challenges. In this chapter, we'll explore some strategies for overcoming obstacles and achieving success.

The first step in overcoming obstacles is to identify the problem. Sometimes, we may be so caught up in the moment that we fail to see the bigger picture. By taking a step back and analyzing the situation, we can gain a better understanding of what's causing the obstacle and how to best address it. Once we've identified the problem, we can begin to develop a plan of action.

One effective strategy for overcoming obstacles is to break them down into smaller, manageable tasks. This can make the challenge feel less overwhelming and more achievable. For example, if you're facing a major project at work, break it down into smaller tasks that can be completed one at a time. This will help you stay focused and motivated, and will also make it easier to measure your progress.

Another important strategy for overcoming obstacles is to stay positive and maintain a can-do attitude. When we're faced with a challenge, it's easy to get discouraged and give up. However, by staying positive and believing in ourselves, we can push through even the toughest of obstacles. This doesn't mean that we should be unrealistic or ignore the difficulties we're facing, but rather that we should approach problems with a sense of optimism and determination.

It's also crucial to seek out support and guidance when facing obstacles. Whether it's a mentor, a friend, or a family member, having someone to talk to and share your thoughts and feelings with can make a big difference. They can provide valuable perspective and help you stay motivated during difficult times.

Another helpful way to overcome obstacles is to learn from our mistakes and failures. We all make mistakes, but it's important to take the time to reflect on what went wrong and how we can improve in the future. By learning from our failures, we can avoid making the same mistakes again and become better equipped to handle similar challenges in the future.

Finally, it's important to remember that overcoming obstacles takes time and effort. There are no quick fixes or easy solutions. However, by staying focused, staying positive, and seeking out support, we can push through even the toughest of challenges and achieve our goals.

In conclusion, overcoming obstacles is an essential part of life. By identifying the problem, breaking it down into smaller tasks, staying positive, seeking support, learning from mistakes and being persistent, we can overcome any obstacle that comes our way. Remember, every obstacle is an opportunity to grow and become a stronger and more resilient person. So, don't give up and keep pushing forward towards success.

CHAPTER EIGHT

Building resilience

Building resilience is the ability to bounce back from difficult situations and challenges. It is a key component in overcoming obstacles and achieving success. Resilience is not something that we are born with, it's something that we can develop and strengthen over time. Here are some strategies for building resilience:

Practice self-care: Taking care of ourselves physically, emotionally and mentally is key to building resilience. This includes getting enough sleep, eating well, exercising, and finding ways to manage stress.

Develop a growth mindset: Having a growth mindset means that we believe we can grow and improve, even in the face of adversity. Instead of giving up when faced with a challenge, we approach it with a sense of determination and the belief that we can overcome it.

Seek support: Building a strong support system is important for building resilience. This can include family, friends, or professionals. These people can offer a listening ear, provide perspective, and offer practical advice.

Learn from mistakes: Failure is a natural part of life, and it is important to learn from our mistakes. When we make a mistake, we should take the time to reflect on what went wrong and how we can improve in the future.

Be proactive: Building resilience is about being proactive, not reactive. Instead of waiting for problems to arise, we can take steps to prevent them from happening in the first place. This includes setting goals, making plans, and taking action.

Practice gratitude: Focusing on the positive things in our lives can help to build resilience. Expressing gratitude for the things we have, rather than dwelling on what we lack, can help to put things in perspective and boost our mood.

Find meaning and purpose: Having a sense of purpose and meaning in our lives can be a powerful source of resilience. It can help to give us a sense of direction and motivation, even in the face of adversity.

In conclusion, building resilience is an ongoing process that requires time, effort and practice. By taking care of ourselves, developing a growth mindset, seeking support, learning from mistakes, being proactive, practicing gratitude, and finding meaning and purpose, we can build the resilience we need to overcome obstacles and achieve success. Remember, resilience is not a one-time achievement, it's a constant work in progress.

CHAPTER NINE

The importance of continued self-discovery and growth.

Self-discovery and growth are essential for personal development and overall well-being. The process of self-discovery is about understanding who we are, what we believe in, and what we want out of life. It helps us to gain a deeper understanding of our strengths, weaknesses, values, and passions. By engaging in self-discovery, we can identify and pursue our goals, aspirations, and passions with more clarity, direction and purpose.

On the other hand, growth is about developing and improving ourselves, both mentally and emotionally. It's about learning new skills, gaining knowledge, and expanding our abilities. It's about pushing ourselves out of our comfort zones, taking risks, and facing challenges. By actively engaging in growth, we can become more self-aware, confident, and capable.

Continued self-discovery and growth are important because they help us to become the best versions of ourselves. It helps us to live a more fulfilling and meaningful life, and to make positive contributions to the world. When we're actively engaged in self-discovery and growth, we're more resilient, adaptable, and capable of overcoming obstacles.

Furthermore, self-discovery and growth are essential for maintaining a positive mindset and outlook on life. When we're stuck in a rut, or feeling stuck, self-discovery and growth can help us to break out of it and see things in a new light. It can help us to see the bigger picture and to find new perspectives, which can be essential for problem-solving and decision-making.

In conclusion, self-discovery and growth are ongoing processes that require commitment and effort. By actively engaging in self-discovery and growth, we can become the best versions of ourselves, live a more fulfilling and meaningful life, and make positive contributions to the world. Remember, self-discovery and growth are not destinations, but rather a journey, and it's important to be open to the opportunities that come your way and to continue learning and growing throughout your life.

CHAPTER TEN

How yoga helps in self discovery?

Yoga is an ancient practice that can be a valuable tool for self-discovery. Yoga combines physical postures, breathing exercises, and meditation to help individuals to connect with their bodies, minds, and spirits.

One of the main benefits of yoga is that it helps to increase self-awareness. By focusing on the breath and the movement of the body, yoga practitioners can become more aware of their thoughts, feelings, and sensations. This increased self-awareness can help individuals to gain a deeper understanding of themselves and their patterns of behavior.

Yoga also helps to reduce stress and anxiety, both of which can be major obstacles in the journey of self-discovery. The physical postures and breathing exercises of yoga can help to release tension and bring a sense of calm to the mind and body. This can help individuals to feel more balanced and centered, which can make it easier to explore one's thoughts and feelings.

In addition, yoga can also help to build resilience and inner strength. The physical postures of yoga can be challenging, and by pushing ourselves out of our comfort zones, we can build the mental and physical strength to overcome obstacles and challenges. This inner strength can also be useful when facing difficult emotions or situations during self-discovery journey.

Yoga can also help to improve overall well-being, which is essential for self-discovery. The practice can help to improve physical health, such as flexibility, strength, and balance, as well as emotional and mental well-being. This can help to create a foundation of balance and well-being, which can make it easier to explore one's thoughts and feelings.

In conclusion, yoga is a valuable tool for self-discovery. By combining physical postures, breathing exercises, and meditation, yoga can help individuals to increase self-awareness, reduce stress and anxiety, build resilience and inner strength, and improve overall well-being. It's an holistic approach that can help to create a foundation of balance and well-being, which can make it easier to explore one's thoughts and feelings. Remember, everyone's self-discovery journey is unique, and it's important to find the practices that work best for you.

CHAPTER ELEVEN

Mindfulness

Mindfulness is the practice of being present and aware of one's thoughts, feelings, and surroundings. It is a key component in the journey of self-discovery, as it helps to increase self-awareness and provide a deeper understanding of oneself.

There are many ways to practice mindfulness, including meditation, yoga, and journaling. One popular form of mindfulness meditation is called "mindful breathing." This involves focusing one's attention on the sensation of breathing, without trying to change or control the breath. This can help to bring a sense of calm and clarity to the mind.

Mindfulness can also be incorporated into daily activities, such as eating, walking, and even showering. The key is to be present in the moment and to focus on the sensations and experiences of the activity. This can help to bring a sense of awareness and appreciation to everyday experiences and can help to reduce stress and anxiety.

Mindfulness has been shown to have many benefits, including reducing stress and anxiety, improving focus and concentration, and increasing self-awareness and self-compassion. It can also help to improve overall well-being and can lead to a deeper understanding of oneself.

It's important to note that mindfulness is a skill that takes practice and patience to develop. It's not something that can be achieved overnight. It's important to approach the practice with a sense of curiosity and non-judgment, and to be gentle with oneself when the mind wanders.

In conclusion, mindfulness is a powerful tool for self-discovery and personal growth. It can help to increase self-awareness, reduce stress, and improve overall well-being. By incorporating mindfulness into daily activities and by being present in the moment, we can gain a deeper understanding of ourselves and our place in the world. Remember, mindfulness is a skill that takes time and practice to develop, be patient and kind with yourself during the journey of self-discovery.

CHAPTER TWELVE

Additional resources and tools to continue the journey of self-discovery.

There are many resources and tools available to help continue the journey of self-discovery. Here are a few examples:

Journaling: Keeping a journal is a great way to explore your thoughts, feelings, and experiences. It can help you to gain insight into your beliefs, values, and motivations.

Therapy: Talking to a therapist or counselor can be a valuable tool for self-discovery. They can provide a safe and confidential space to explore your thoughts and feelings and offer guidance and support.

Self-help books: There are a wide variety of self-help books available on a range of topics related to self-discovery and personal growth. Reading these books can help to provide new perspectives and inspiration for personal growth.

Personal Development workshops and courses: Many communities, organizations and educational institutions offer personal development workshops and courses that can help to provide tools and strategies to support personal growth.

Mindfulness and meditation: Mindfulness and meditation practices can help to increase self-awareness, reduce stress, and promote a sense of inner peace and calm.

Self-Reflection: Taking time to reflect on your thoughts and actions can help you to gain a better understanding of yourself and make positive changes in your life.

Coaching: Life coaches are trained to help individuals identify and achieve their goals by providing guidance, support, and accountability.

Travel: Traveling to new places and experiencing new cultures can be a powerful tool for self-discovery. It can help to broaden our perspectives and help us to learn more about ourselves and the world around us.

Hobbies and interests: Engaging in hobbies and interests that align with our passions and values can also be a great way to learn more about ourselves.

It's important to keep in mind that self-discovery is a personal journey and different tools and resources may work better for some people than others. It's important to find the tools and resources that work best for you and to be open to trying new things. Also, remember that self-discovery is an ongoing process and it's important to continue to explore and learn about yourself throughout your life.

Glossary

Here is a list of terms that could be used in a book about the art of self-discovery and their definitions:

- Self-discovery: The process of learning about oneself, including one's strengths, weaknesses, values, and passions.
- Personal growth: The process of developing and improving oneself, both mentally and emotionally.
- Mindfulness: The practice of being present and aware of one's thoughts, feelings, and surroundings.
- Journaling: The practice of keeping a written record of one's thoughts, feelings, and experiences.
- Therapy: The process of working with a trained professional to explore one's thoughts, feelings, and behaviors in order to gain insight and make positive changes.
- Self-help books: Books that provide advice and strategies for personal growth and self-improvement.
- Personal development workshops: Groups or classes that provide tools and strategies to support personal growth.
- Meditation: A practice in which an individual uses a technique – such as mindfulness or focusing the mind on a particular object, thought, or activity – to train attention and awareness, and achieve a mentally clear and emotionally calm and stable state.
- Coaching: A process of guiding individuals or groups in order to help them identify and achieve their goals.
- Reflection: The process of thinking about and reviewing one's experiences, beliefs, and actions in order to gain

new insights and understandings.
- Resilience: The ability to bounce back from difficult situations and challenges.
- Growth mindset: The belief that one can grow and improve, even in the face of adversity.
- Self-care: The practice of taking care of oneself, including physical, emotional and mental well-being.
- Support system: A network of people who offer support, guidance, and encouragement, including family, friends, and professionals.
- Purpose: The reason or reasons for which something is done or created or for which something exists.
- Authenticity: Being true to oneself and one's values, rather than trying to be someone else or conform to societal expectations.

www.ingramcontent.com/pod-product-compliance
Lightning Source LLC
Chambersburg PA
CBHW030507170726
47990CB00008BA/3081